10 Day Green Smoothie Cleanse

Delicious Smoothie Recipes To Shed 15+ Pounds In 10 Days

D1551672

© Michelle Bakeman

Disclaimer

Table of Contents

Introduction

Hi there,

I'm Michelle Bakeman. Nice to meet you!

Are you tired of trying useless diets in an effort to get healthy and lose weight? Well, so am I.

That is why I have compiled a recipe book filled with delicious smoothies to help you shed up to 15+ pounds in just 10 days!

Say goodbye to silly diets and cleanse your body. You will feel healthier, more energetic, lose weight, and even reduce food cravings.

10 days begin now, let's get started!

- Michelle Bakeman

Spinach Avocado Smoothie

<u>Ingredients</u> –

- 1 ½ cups of apple juice

- 2 cups of stemmed and some chopped spinach/kale

- 1 apple that is cored, chopped and unpeeled

- ½ chopped avocado

<u>Directions</u> –

1. Mix all of the apple juice, apples, spinach, and the avocado in your blender while pureeing it until it is smooth.

2. Do this for about 1 minute
    while adding water to get
    the level you want.

3. Chill.

4. Serve and enjoy!

Emerald Smoothie

Ingredients –

- 4 ounces of low fat vanilla yogurt

- 2 cups of fresh and ripe pineapples with the cores

- 1 celery stalk that's halved or chopped

- 2 cups of gently packed spinach leaves

- 2 cups of ice cubes

- Sweetener

Directions –

1. Place all of the ingredients inside of your blender while processing it.

2. Chill it.

3. Serve and enjoy!

Key Lime Smoothie

Ingredients –

- 1/4th cup of water

- 1 tablespoon of key lime juice

- 2 medium kiwi's peeled and halved

- 1 large ripe pear that is seeded and halved

- 2 tablespoons of honey

- 1 cup of ice cubes

Directions –

1. Place all of the ingredients inside of your blender while processing it.

2. Chill it.

3. Serve and enjoy!

Spinach Cocktail

Ingredients –

- 1 cup of water

- 2 mint leaves

- 2 cups of fresh spinach leaves

- 1 cup of frozen pineapple chunks

Directions –

1. Place all of the ingredients inside of your blender while processing it.

2. Chill it.

3.   Serve and enjoy!

Kale Pear Smoothie

Ingredients –

- 1 cup of water

- 1 cup of green grapes

- 1 orange that's been halved and peeled

- ½ ripe pear halved and seeded

- 1 small peeled banana

- 1 cup of kale

- 2 cups of ice cubes

Directions –

1. Place all of the ingredients
    inside of your blender
    while processing it.

2. Chill it.

3. Serve and enjoy!

Peach Green Smoothie

Ingredients –

- 1 cup of soy milk

- 2 cups of lightly packed fresh spinach

- 1 medium apple seeded and quartered

- 2 cups of frozen and unsweetened peach slices

Directions –

1. Place all of the ingredients inside of your blender while processing it.

2. Chill it.

3.   Serve and enjoy!

Monster Smoothie

<u>Ingredients</u> –

- 1 large peeled and segmented orange

- ½ of a large banana that's cut into various chunks

- 6 large strawberries

- 2 cups of spinach

- 1/3rd cup of plain Greek yogurt

- 1 cup of ice

<u>Directions</u> –

1. Place all of the ingredients inside of your blender while processing it.

2. Chill it.

3. Serve and enjoy!

Strawberry Kale

Ingredients –

- 3/4th bottle of water

- 2 cups of kale with no stems

- 1 pint of strawberries

- 1 apple

- 1 banana

Directions –

1. Place all of the ingredients inside of your blender while processing it.

2. Chill it.

3.   Serve and enjoy!

Honeydew Romaine Smoothie

Ingredients –

- 4 cups of honeydew

- 11 leafs of romaine lettuce

- Cup of water

Directions –

1. Place all of the ingredients inside of your blender while processing it.

2. Chill it.

3. Serve and enjoy!

Watermelon Kale

Ingredients –

- 5 cups of watermelon

- 1 cup of kale

- Water

Directions –

1. Place all of the ingredients inside of your blender while processing it.

2. Chill it.

3. Serve and enjoy!

Sweet & Sour Smoothie

Ingredients –

- 4 apricots

- 2/3rd head of red leaf lettuce

- 2 ounces of blueberries

- 2 cups of water

- 1 cup of banana

Directions –

1. Place all of the ingredients
    inside of your blender
    while processing it.

2. Chill it.

3. Serve and enjoy!

Summer Smoothie

Ingredients –

- 5 cups of spinach

- 2 cups of peaches

- 2 cups of water

- 1 cup of mango

Directions –

1. Place all of the ingredients inside of your blender while processing it.

2. Chill it.

3.   Serve and enjoy!

Raspberry Spinach Smoothie

Ingredients –

- 10 ounces of spinach

- 1 cup of apples

- 1 cup of raspberries

- 1 ½ cups of water

- 1 banana

Directions –

1. Place all of the ingredients inside of your blender while processing it.

2. Chill it.

3. Serve and enjoy!

Simple Smoothie

Ingredients –

- 5 cups of watermelon

- 3 ½ cups of kale

Directions –

1. Place all of the ingredients inside of your blender while processing it.

2. Chill it.

3. Serve and enjoy!

Purple Smoothie

<u>Ingredients</u> –

- 8 leaves of Swiss chard

- 2 cups of blackberries

- 1 cup of grapes

- 1 cup of water

- 1 apple

- 1 banana

<u>Directions</u> –

1. Place all of the ingredients
    inside of your blender
    while processing it.

2. Chill it.

3. Serve and enjoy!

Pineapple Surprise

Ingredients –

- 2 dandelion greens

- 2 cups of water

- ½ cup of strawberries

- 1 cup of pineapples

- 1 banana

Directions –

1. Place all of the ingredients inside of your blender while processing it.

2.   Chill it.

3.   Serve and enjoy!

Green Pineapple Fruit

Ingredients –

- 5 leaves of Swiss chard

- 1 cup of starfruit

- 1 cup of pineapples

- 1 cup of water

- 1 banana

Directions –

1. Place all of the ingredients inside of your blender while processing it.

2. Chill it.

3. Serve and enjoy!

Spinach Papaya

Ingredients –

- Juice from ½ of an orange

- 2 cups of papayas

- 1 cup of water

- 1 bunch of spinach

Directions –

1. Place all of the ingredients inside of your blender while processing it.

2. Chill it.

3.   Serve and enjoy!

Parsley Kiwi Smoothie

Ingredients –

- 2 peeled Kiwi's

- 2 cups of parsley

- 2 cups of water

- 1 apple

- 1 banana

Directions –

1. Place all of the ingredients inside of your blender while processing it.

2. Chill it.

3. Serve and enjoy!

Cucumber Smoothie

Ingredients –

- 1 juice from orange

- 2 cups of Purslane

- 2 pears

- ½ cup of water

- 1 cucumber

Directions –

1.   Place all of the ingredients
     inside of your blender
     while processing it.

2.   Chill it.

3.   Serve and enjoy!

CPSIA information can be obtained
at www.ICGtesting.com
Printed in the USA
LVOW04s2346200516

489248LV00021B/1014/P